I AM THE UNIVERSE

I AM THE UNIVERSE

PALLAVI VARMA

ZORBA BOOKS

ZORBA BOOKS

Published by Zorba Books, June 2023
Website: www.zorbabooks.com
Email: info@zorbabooks.com

Title: **I am the Universe**
Author Name: Pallavi Varma
Copyright © Pallavi Varma
Printbook ISBN :- 978-93-95217-78-1
Ebook ISBN :- 978-93-95217-77-4

Zorba Books Pvt. Ltd. (opc)
Sushant Arcade,
Next to Courtyard Marriot,
Sushant Lok 1, Gurgaon – 122009, India

Printed by Manipal Technologies Limited
A1 & A2 Shivalli Industrial Area Manipal Udupi, Karnataka – 576104

For my nanaji...

Preface

'A caged parrot', my first poetry prompt, given to me on a balmy summer afternoon by my nanaji, as we sat in the veranda overlooking the courtyard, sipping the 'bel sharbat' my nani had just served us. I had rearranged a few cliches to form a rather insipid rhyming verse and had passed on the notepad to him.

"*Bahut badhiya!*" he had exclaimed, as he always did on everyone's achievement, however little and insignificant they might have been.

He always donned the cape of an encourager, wielding his words like a superhero, casting beams of praise and captivating the attention of all who bore witness to his uplifting words.

And as it did to everyone, his words had engulfed me like a gentle breeze on that sunny afternoon. Right when the buoyant sunlight was filling up the shrivelled courtyard, his words of encouragement had come as a shimmering light that ignited a novel spark in the 12-year-old me.

And so began my journey of writing.

A journey that bears witness to handwritten symphony of dreams, aspirations and heartfelt musings. A journey where imagination intertwines with experiences, passing through the sepia toned fields of nostalgia, basking in the amber glow of renewed consciousness.

As I extend an invitation to you to come venture into the kaleidoscope of my odyssey, I know Nanaji is holding a copy too.

"Bahut badhiya!" I can hear the stars whispering.

Introduction

You, dear reader, are the universe.

Swimming in your eyes are a million stars, some shimmering with hope; lighting up the dark throes of your soul, some dead, flickering with the memories of the past that is still trapped inside their burnt cores. On a warm evening, the sparkle in your eyes illuminate the dull earth. On a cold night, those listless eyes, carrying the weight of dead imprisoned stars, envelopes your soul's girth.

The eyes mirror the vastness of the sky and the mysteries of outer realms. Traces of forgotten stardust, the secrets of unexplored galaxies- the eyes hold the helm.

The eyes, your eyes, are the window to the universe.

You, dear reader, are the universe.

Rummaging through rims of your mind are windy thoughts, sometimes wuthering, occasionally breezy, always bustling. Like a wind's whisper on a rainy day, they leave a stain of a misty memory. Like a howling storm in snowy winter, squally thoughts linger, tasting savoury. Scattering seeds of sanguinity and perfusing pleasure are those warm fuzzies just like spring's zephyr.

The thoughts unceasingly susurrate, rustling through the still green surface of mind. Carrying pollens of consciousness from far and wide, they permeate, letting memories be enshrined. Of life, of awareness, of energy, the thoughts, as wind, invariably remind.

The thoughts, your thoughts, are the window to the universe.

You, dear reader, are the universe.

A dense green forest laden with figs and pears or a barren land; crumpled, creased with a tear. Blooming flowers, withering petals, succulent leaves, stinging nettles. A yellow butterfly in search of her nectar or a haunted garden with whooshing spectres. Your heart, as earth, encapsulates it all. It honours the sun and smiles at the moon when the night falls.

Your heart, as earth, endures the storms, holds roots, heals cracks, flourishes while adorning thorns. Like the resilience of a tree, like the strength of a river, like a flower blossoming in all its splendour, is the heart, your heart, as earth, the centre.

The heart, your heart, is the window to the universe.

You, dear reader, are the universe.

Remember the day, dear reader, when a blazing rage burnt down the house of hope you had conscientiously built? Remember the night when your eyes glistened with a smouldering longing, or was it a flickering guilt? That spark when your eyes met a stranger on a sunny afternoon or the burning desire soaking you up in balmy monsoon? Have your sorrows been washed ashore, have the fluttering ripples of love drenched you before?

Emotions, as glittering flame igniting desires; setting dreams aflame, as blazing pyre. Gigantic, turbulent, as an ocean. Wrapping you in tides of tranquillity, are emotions. Crippling yet calming, healing yet scarring, naked yet an armour, as fire, as water.

The emotions, your emotions, are the window to the universe.

You, dear reader, are the universe.

Thou art that.

Tat Tvam Asi.

|| तत्त्वमसि ||

Elements of The Universe

Earth

Her scent wafted on the breeze,
elusive, vibrant, a citrus tease.
She sauntered
like a river strolling to the sea,
unabashed, unapologetic, free.
Rebellious, resilient, exuding power,
she was after all a wildflower.

{A fragrant rebellion}

A deafening silence pierced her soul,
ridges of her heart sighed,
an avalanche of emotions
waiting to unfold.
Mossy hazel eyes bled rime,
crevasses of her lips grew cold.
The longingness deepened,
an ache for someone to hold.
For someone to caress,
for someone to embrace
the secrets she withholds;
in her slopes, in her folds.
She resigns; for her fate is foretold.
Solitude is the price she pays,
the price for touching the sky,
alone and unopposed.

{Veiled peaks of solitude}

The dried dandelions
defy fate, destined to bloom
from their dwindling death.

{Transcendental dandelions}

One last gaze,
through cataracts of snow,
a blurry enchantment,
ashen hazed glow.
The old man sighs,
sounds of frigid ballet,
alabaster life surmised,
bleached beard sways.

A spot of silky lavender
settles on his frosty robe.
Moisty moss creeps,
anchored on dainty lobes.
Golden light beckons,
whispering final farewell,
he draws a veil, rests
knowing his legacy will swell.

{Winter goes to sleep}

Seeds of solitude,
strewn in sulphate soil,
soaked in sinister salt,
sprouts a sonnet.
Shades spirit scarlet.

{Sprouting solace}

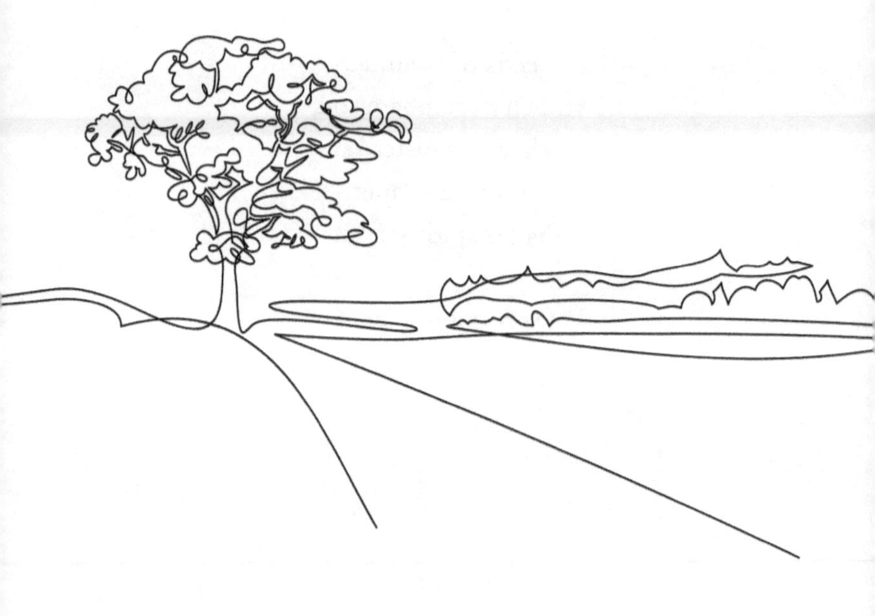

O Shepherd my Shepherd,
take me
to the greener grass,
find me
my mystic spot,
where,
rivers sparkle,
swans dance,
where,
you can put me
into a deep trance.
O Shepherd my Shepherd,
lead me to my destiny.

{The wayward sheep}

Whirling glitters in veins,
choking on fireflies,
she glows in the dark,
under the burnt orange skies.
Liquid moonbeams whisper love,
crimson with conversations of stars above.
Cicada symphony illuminates the night,
wilting daisies now blossom in moonlight.

{The cosmic conversations}

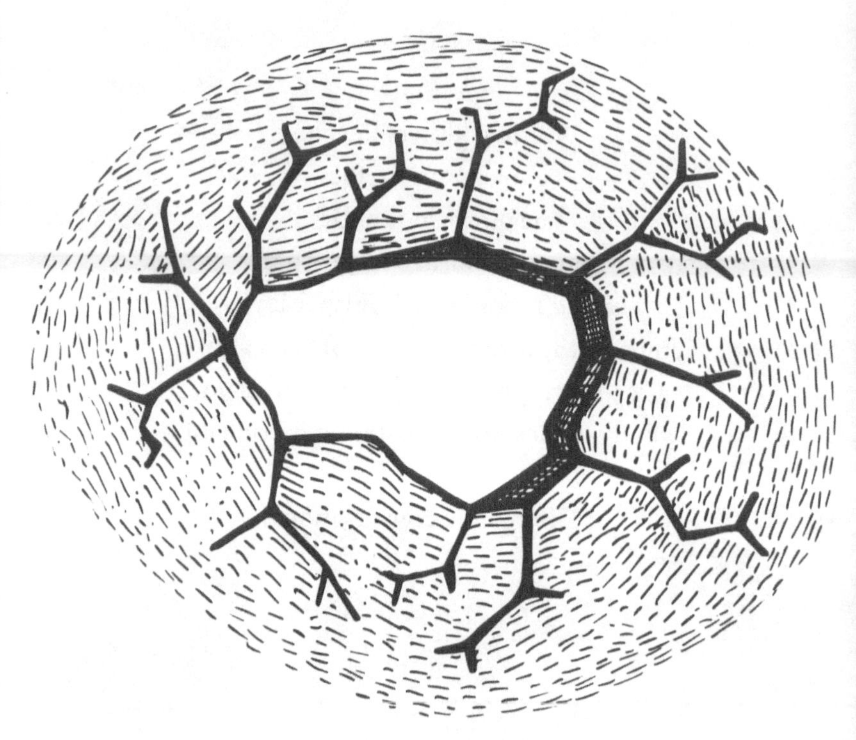

Sun's deceptive grin,
cracked open earth's concealed wounds.
A wildflower blooms.

{Beauty of brokenness}

She smelt of dried dandelions,
her eyes, a shade autumn.
She sauntered like lost fireflies,
her soul, fiery atoms.

She whispered like a wildfire,
her hair, luscious grey clouds.
She smiled like a summer noon,
her touch, as lightening shrouds.

She looked over my shoulder,
standing still in all her glory.
Embracing me like a lost love
was anxiety,
the protagonist of my poetry.

{The wildfire whisperer}

Shaking with fury,
she unleashes her fierce wrath.
Rivers change their path.

{A mother's wrath}

Her nurturing womb,
life's tapestry woven deep,
cradled love endowed.

Her steadfast heart beats,
unyielding in face of pain.
Undaunted, unbowed.

{Mother nurture}

The sun didn't shine on me,
I bloomed in melancholic nights.
My heart is not made of flowers,
it's made of grit, will and might

{The midnight bloomer}

Soft pulse of the morning breeze,
murmur of eucalyptus trees,
whispers of shimmering seas,
The calmness, the tranquillity, the peace.

Glistening of the morning dew,
vastness of sky that's blue,
rhythmic flowers dancing on cue,
The effervescence, the vivacity, the hues.

Blossoming of daisies in spring,
chirping when birds sing,
joyous, mighty flight of wings,
The sacred play, the symphony, the divine strings.

{Nature's serenade}

Beyond this golden gate
there is a vast meadow,
of sunflowers and sunshine,
of blue moon and glittering skyline,
of humming birds and rainbows,
of glistening river and sparkling snow,
of selfless love and serenity,
of infinite light and cosmic divinity.
Beyond this golden gate
our love will thrive with dignity,
I will meet you there my love,
at the horizon of eternity.

{Where I am infinity}

Sky

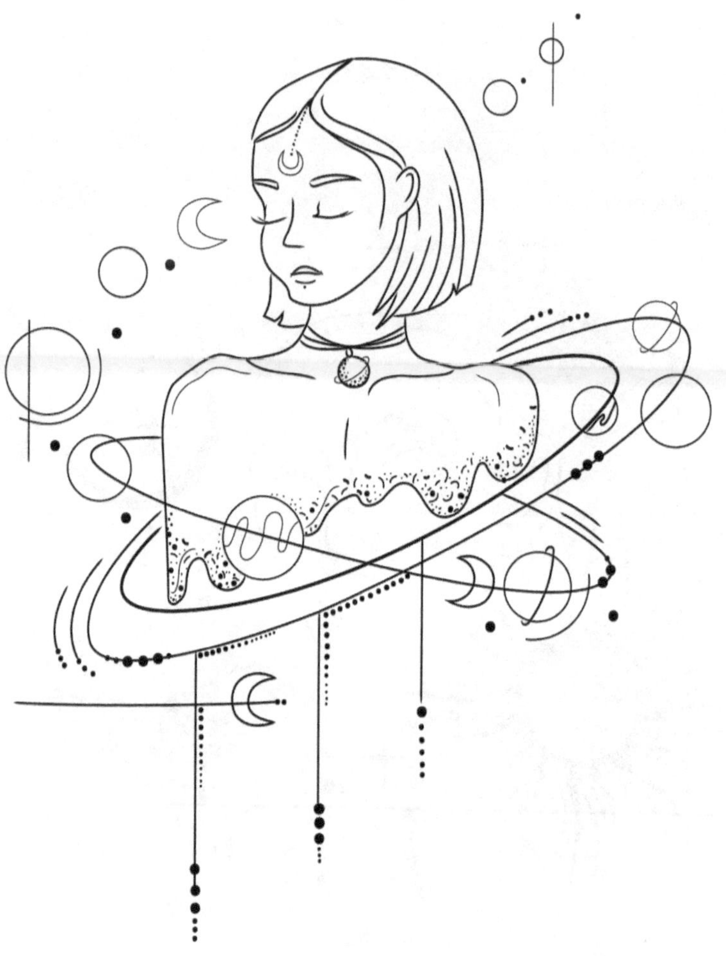

She is made of
stardust and moonbeams,
holding constellations in her arms.
Poetry woven in her soul,
she pulls galaxies with her charm.
Sun wrapped on her fingers,
jewelled moon in her palm.
She commands the depths of space,
balmy spirit radiating calm.
Dare not fall in love though,
for she is busy owning her glow.

{Queen of the cosmos}

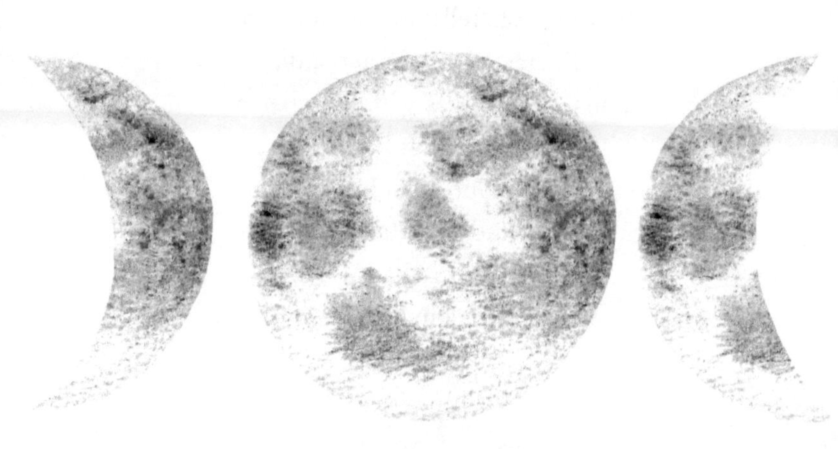

Thousand scars adorned,
I wander with the stars,
adrift and forlorn.

{The nomadic moon}

The skies were tainted with her tears,
night, pregnant with her grief,
clouds hid in despair,
stormy winds heaved,
stars had witnessed the suffering
of moon's eternal yearning
for the sun,
since the universe was spun.

{Universe's unrequited love}

Our long-distance love was
a tale for the gospel,
you were a star in the sky
and I, a mere mortal.

{The eternal divide}

Moon undressed the snow,
painting the gaunt winter flakes
with silver starlight.

{A winter romance}

(S)himmering sea
(U)nder glittering sky
(N)ourishing silence
(S)oaking in delight
(H)eaving waves
(I)lluminating bright
(N)avigating silhouette is
(E)bullient sunlight

{The illuminated path}

Blood moon peeped,
inundating me with its crimson light,
as your parched fangs had pierced me,
sucked my soul, drenched in gore,
on that dark intoxicating night.

{Crimson intoxication}

Magical fireflies
weave ethereal stories,
ignites night's glory.

{Sparkling storytellers of the dark}

Wilted withered wings,
hold dreams on a broken hinge,
still soaring the sky.

{Triumph of the soul}

Skies turned grey,
woods, a shade black,
palm trees frayed away,
lilac roses, ruined and wracked
stars, dimmed their ray,
blue waves, stormed and crashed,
moon, dulled in dismay,
yellow lightening, raged and splashed.
Nature, an enraged lover;
his fury, unmasked

{Chaos in the Kingdom}

Sun spilled some sunshine,
stroking the Cosmo's canvas.
Summer shimmers, shines.

{The divine intervention}

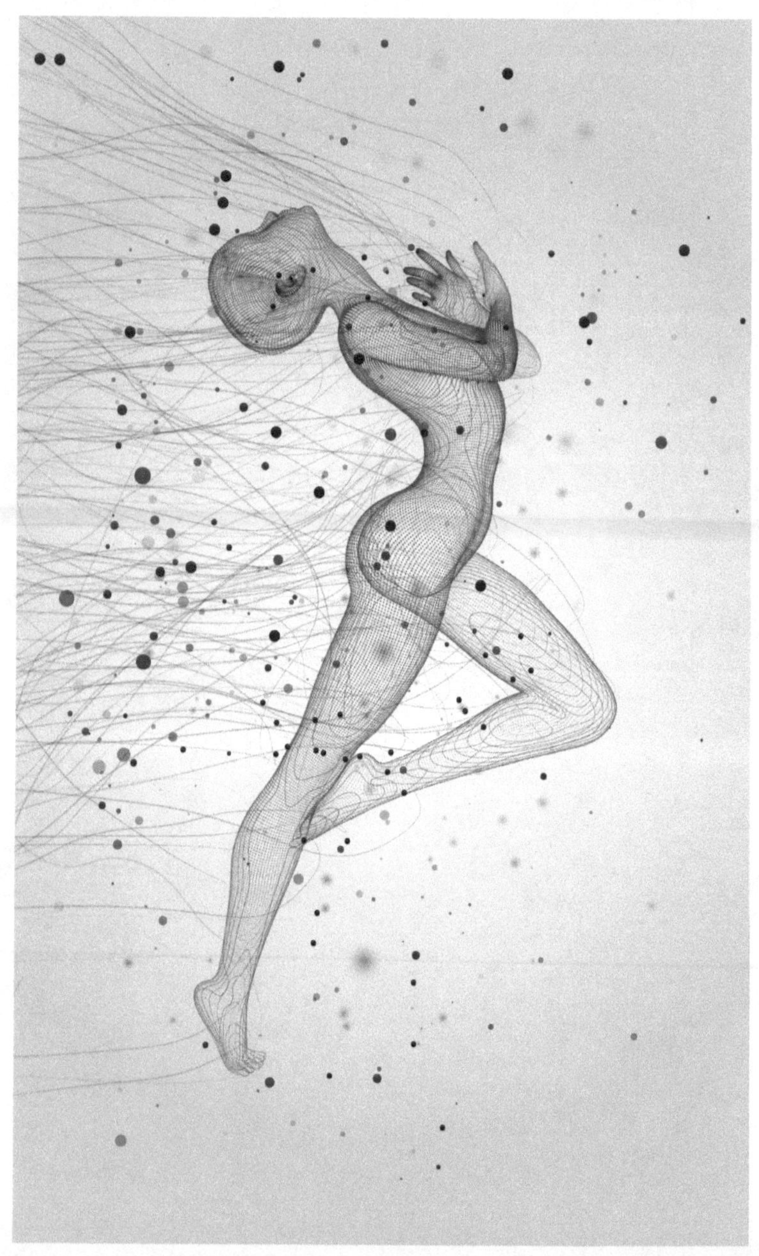

She had longed for a home,
yearned for a safe-place
to call her own.
She looked for it in his arms,
sought solace in faraway farms.
Rummaged scattered memories,
searched for it in old melodies.
Scurried hither thither,
for a resting place
and finally found it
with sky's warm embrace.

{The homecoming}

Draped in a cotton candy pink
and misty silver pearls,
she glistens with exuberance,
with her new-born she twirls.
Brushing stardust upon his face,
she marvels at his crescent glow,
whispering celestial lullabies
envelopes him in her silken chateau.

Time spins gently, as it does
he blooms as she silently weathers.
An heir to the magnificent sky,
he ascends to his throne
and she, to nether

Sky dwellers hail, his praise they bespeak,
crown him, the moon, lord of mystique.
Pregnant with pride, glee enwrapped,
she breaks into a joyous thunderclap.
Tears falls from her gleaming eye,
she, the cloud, bursts into swirls of delight.
Ah! the reason of her demise.

{Moonlit motherhood}

Sky's changing colours,
indigo to sombre grey.
Have birds gone astray?

{A Mother's Watchful Eye}

Wind

Whistling wind wails,
Wandering through wizened woods,
Witness to time's tales.

{Stories of time}

Angelic embrace,
sacred dance and cosmic verse.
Rhythmic universe.

Celestial choreographer
dancing through the fields,
to the symphony he leads.
Hums of jingles,
murmurs of hymns,
brimming with joy within.
In his melody, I immerse.
Rhythmic universe.

{The cosmic rhapsody}

On the banks of an ethereal river
under the bur flower tree,
he twirls with the cherubs
with exuberant abandon
and euphoric glee.

A whiff of his gleaming glimmer
caresses my fragile soul,
he expands,
as I beguile him with extolls.
I long for his company,
I long to own him whole.

An Ephemeral lover, he withers,
scented memory slithers.
My spirit he scours,
He, the transcendental wind
I merely a mortal flower.
On his notes, I simply sway
I am just a fleeting embrace
in his sacred play

{The divine at play}

Wild wind whispers,
sharing secrets with the leaves.
Wildflowers whimper.

{A wildflower's envy}

Chasing butterflies under the afternoon sun,
the inhibited laughter, no worries to shun.
Running wild, jumping fences,
living with abandon, no pretences.
Dancing in puddles, soaking in the rain,
the echoes of memories remain.
Its souvenirs, on my mind, still pinned
Ah! my childhood,
gone with the wind.

{Memories in the breeze}

A broken feather drift downwards,
like a white shadow
descending to doom.
Embraced by a treacherous breeze.

{Lost in the Wind}

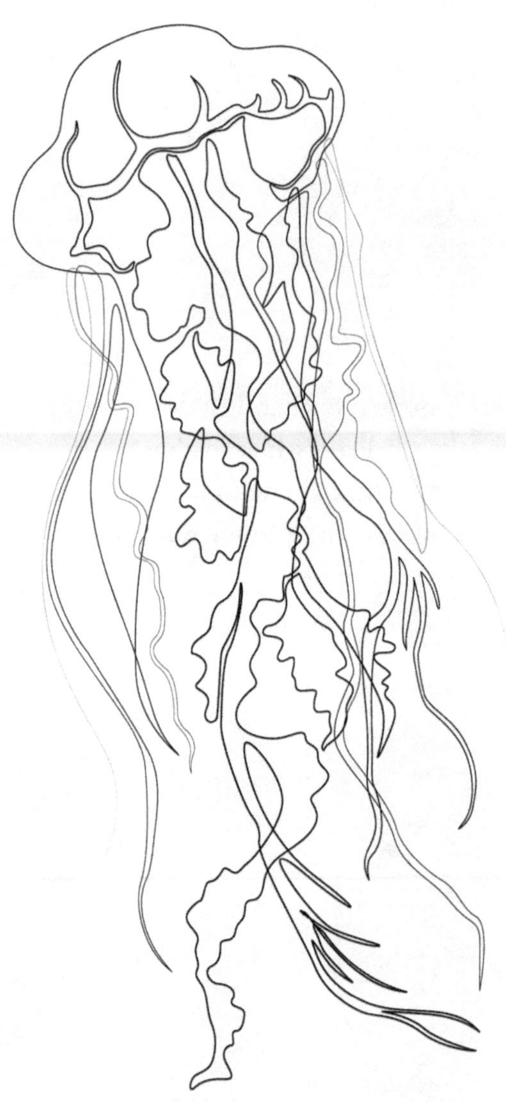

Untangled knots of past,
caressed silhouettes of my heart,
whispered secrets only the wind knew,
faded away like morning dew.
Just a beautiful nightmare,
darling! why can't you be true?

{The illusion of truth}

Quivering at its very sight
I sit frightened at my ivory bedside,
what was a gentle zephyr in the day,
had turned to a stormy cyclone by night,
smothering me with all its might,
your love, my darling, a brutal blight
on my body, on my soul, on my life.
Consuming me, until I was no more
than a ghostly light.

{The hurricane of heartbreak}

Teapot tempest brews,
fury swirls like boiling tea,
spilling over brims.

{Boiling Point}

I had held
in my palms
the grains of
woes and qualms.
As twilight alights,
these grains slip by,
I return to my nest
with a twinkle in my eye.
The winds of light,
hold my hand
as I sprinkle these
grains of sand.

{The winds of light}

Fire

Dressed in satanic sins,
I dance with my demons,
to chase a fire within.

{Dance of the damned}

I burn in despair
embers on skin, he rescues
with a kiss of death.

{From embers to eternity}

Dressed in sins,
embers on skin,
I ascend to heaven,
my beloved beckons.
There are tales to tell,
memories to dwell,
a few bones to pick
for his mischievous tricks.
Drenched in delight,
I embrace my date night.

{A heavenly courtship}

Mourning in a morgue,
half drenched visceral desires.
I light the wet pyre.

{The smouldering remains}

That flame I saw in your eyes,
now burns up the evening sky.
An inferno sphere, a poet's delight,
the blues turn to a searing light.
Birds run awry, sun retreats,
as your blazing soul fiercely leads.

{Fire in the sky}

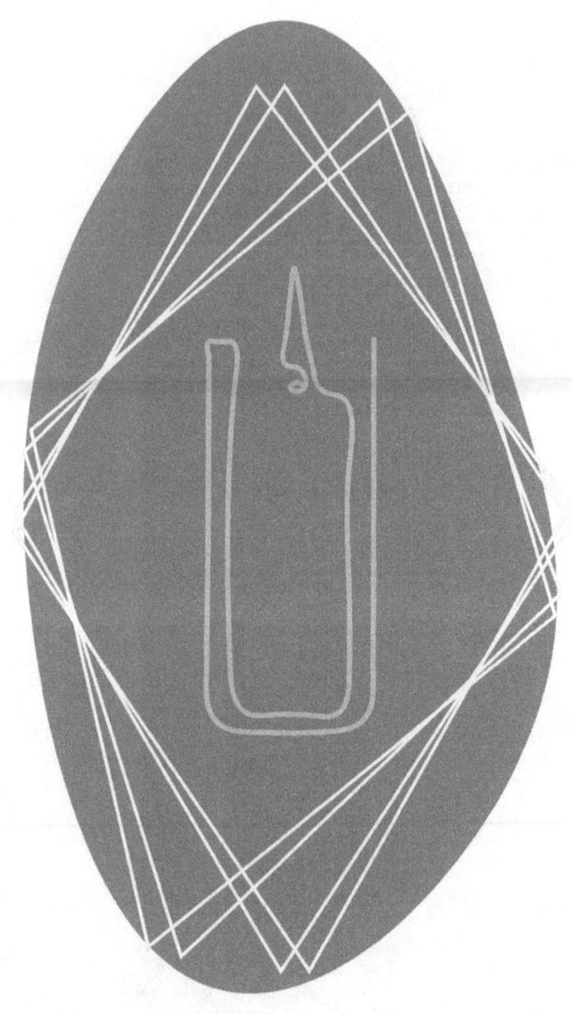

The last flame flickers,
dancing to the beat of death.
Darkness heaves for breath

{The final flicker}

Ashes of my heart
that you had carelessly tossed,
smouldered with grim ire,
metamorphosing into
a wild untamed forest fire.

{Blaze of betrayal}

Cinders simmer
under my skin,
as your lips
chart a path,
setting fire
to my carnal sins.
A sweet melancholy,
our souls
strum,
in its heat
I succumb.

{Skin on fire}

She tiptoed at break of dawn,
I had waited for so long,
staring in the abyss, adrift and forlorn.

She whispered a sweet lullaby,
setting me free from treacheries and lies.
I embraced her like a lost firefly.

She hushed, kissed with delight,
those twinkling eyes, guiding to twilight.
She, my death, ignited in me a platinum light.

{Platinum firefly's lullaby}

Golden dripping light,
falls on purple frozen face.
The divine embrace

{Cradled in celestial light}

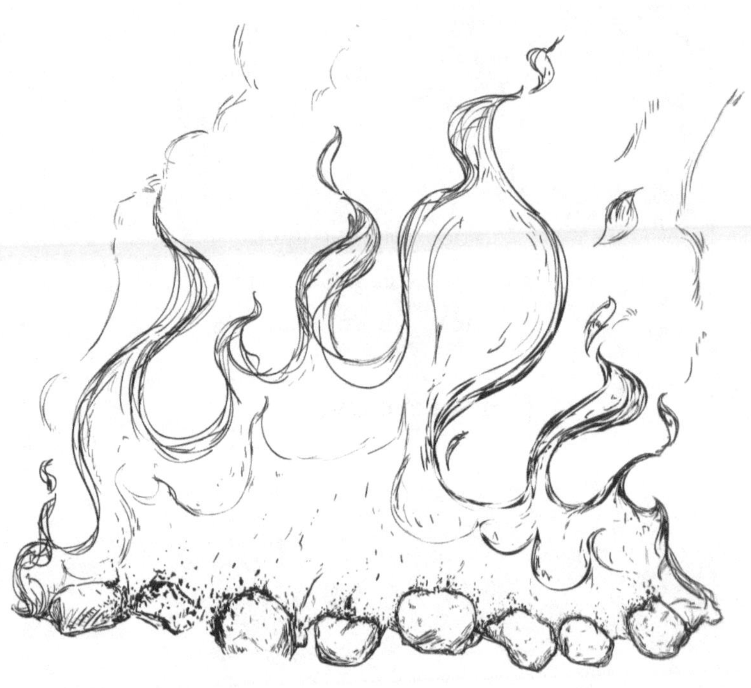

I peel-off burnt dreams,
tossing charred memories to ground,
empty promises flicker
as I torch its mound.
Smokes of past swirl,
embered tears surround,
your cold heart now ablaze,
I am finally unbound.

{A searing inferno}

Water

Rogue river meets the sea,
losing her name,
relinquishing her entity.
Drowns in eternal endless infinity.

{Surrendering to oblivion}

I swim among the sharks,
my dreams ensnared in coral gold,
tied in my tresses are secrets of the sea,
azure waves of the ocean, my eyes behold.

Yet, I yearn for the ebullient sunlight,
summoning me from the distant shore,
to caress the silhouettes of my mind,
to embrace the world, I'm yet to explore.

I yearn for the surface; I yearn to be free,
knowing it eludes, for I am just a mermaid of the sea.

{Tresses of the sea}

Stormy wave to my pristine shore,
enticing, turbulent, ripping through my core.
You brought apprehensions & anguish galore,
leaving me murkier than before.

{Troubled waters}

A splash of rainbow
A knock by splattering rain
Is that love again?

{Rainy rekindling}

Clouded doubts loomed over,
drowning me in screams.
Sliced open my wounds,
untangling seams of my dream.
Thunders revealed the love you feigned,
silver droplets now fall in silence, like rain.

{The thunderous truth}

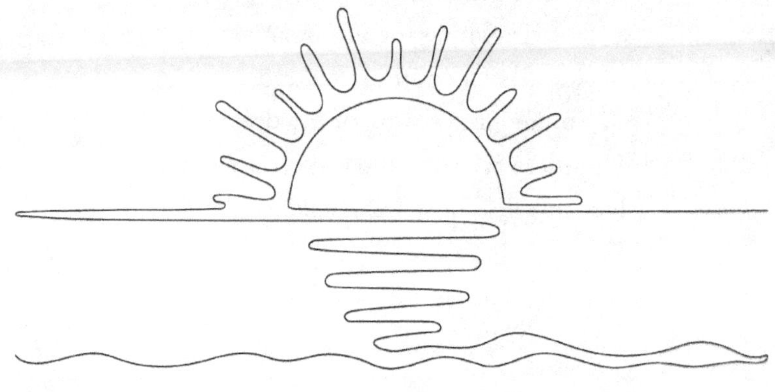

Scattered on ocean,
my share of tepid sunshine.
Bliss soaked in some brine.

{Salty serenity}

Walked barefoot in murky meadow,
her pristine heart befouled with grime.
Prickly peonies murmured,
solitary pines chimed.
Pierced her soul crimson,
white dreams now dime.
She, snowflake,
melted,
dried.

{The fragility of joy}

Whimsical desires
now a tale for folklore.
Porcelain dreams
orphaned on mosaic floor, as
your lifeless eyes washed ashore.

{A tale for folklore}

A lone stream meander,
through the woods, its path unknown.
Like a child astray.

{The rambling rivulet}

The flower pinned to her hair,
was a lovely shade of white,
her cheek, a flush of pink
her eyes, soaked in delight.
The silver gown draping her curves,
shimmered with a lover's pride.
Her bosom rose and fell,
as she glided like poet's recite.

He watched her from afar
his eyes glistening, his jaws pulled wide
his face, sharp edges, soft curves
a heady cocktail of sorrow and excite.
His heart aching for an embrace,
to forever have her on his side.

Ah! but their fates, pre-defined.
A race against time.

She would dwindle, fade away,
the moment they entwined.
Leaving him with shells of memories
as she merges back with divine.
Transient love, enshrined

{Sea and shore}

A barren parched lake,
dusty, arid, desolate,
yearns for a pour,
to quench his deep droughty core.
His dry thirst intensifies.

Drizzles divine grace,
sprinkling of revelation.
A Resurrection.

{The pour within}

In the universe, we merely blend
It's never the end…

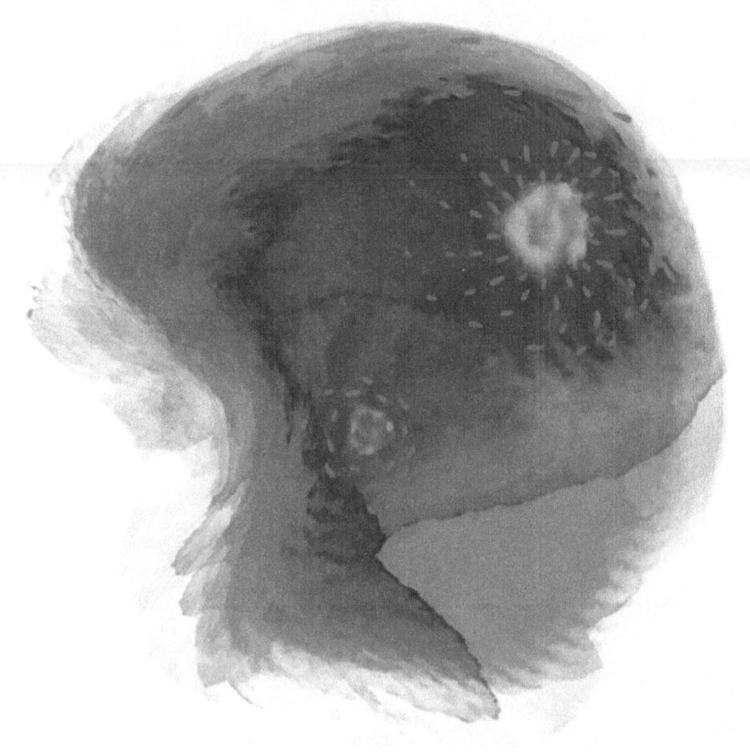

Acknowledgement

Writing is never a solitary pursuit, and this book is no different.

It bears the imprints of everyone I have had the privilege of meeting along my journey of self-discovery. Each encounter, whether fleeting or enduring, has shaped the essence of these poetic verses, infusing them with the colours of human connection and the richness of shared experiences.

To my family, Mummy, Papa and Pranjal, the foundation upon which my creative spirit has flourished, I express my deepest gratitude for your unwavering support, your unconditional love, and of course, your genes!

A special note to the love of our lives, Lucy. There is no one like you. Thank you for filling my heart with so much love and purpose that it brimmed over on the pages of this book.

Immensely grateful to the tender encouragement and unwavering faith and support of my nani, aunts, uncles and cousins.

Shourya, a special thanks to you for being my constant sounding board and incessantly unrumpling the creases of self-doubts that frequently found its abode in my mind.

To my friends, to the fiery sparks, that kindles the sparks of my imagination, my heartfelt appreciation. Your companionship and your conversations have been a safe haven to explore the depths of my thoughts and emotions. I hope you find the imprints of our shared laughter and tears between the pages of this book.

Avneet, Tapeshwari, Pooja, Reshu, Shrestha, a big thank you for being my constant cheerleaders. Your presence in my life is a gift beyond measure.

Manjari and Payal di, thank you for being the beacons in my poetic journey. You are the lighthouse to my wayward poetic ship.

To my publisher, Zorba books, heartfelt gratitude for ensuring a smooth and seamless process. Thank you for bringing my words to life and making my dream a reality.

To the readers, thank you for holding this book in your hands. Your willingness to embark on this journey with me, to delve into the realms of emotion and introspection, fills my heart with joy and purpose. I know in my heart that this is going to be a cherished companionship.

To the Universe itself, thank you for orchestrating the serendipitous encounters and serendipitous moments that have shaped my path. Every interaction, every word of encouragement, and every shared experience has contributed to the tapestry of my creative expression. To all those who have crossed my path, knowingly or unknowingly, I thank you for leaving a lasting imprint on my creative journey.

Eternally grateful.
Pallavi.

About The Author

Raised among the giants of science and medicine and having made a career as a business management professional herself, Pallavi found an unexpected confidant in art. Born in Gaya, Bihar, a city steeped in enlightenment and salvation, she was shaped by devotion and a belief in divine interventions. The decades spent living in various cities across the country enriched her with a treasure trove of experiences and a deep understanding of intricate human emotions.

When not immersed in work or writing, she can be found curled beside Lucy, the center of her universe.

This marks Pallavi's debut book, a testament to her journey and unwavering spirit.

You can reach out to Pallavi on:
https://www.instagram.com/writingg.out.loud/
pallavii.varmaa@gmail.com